FRESH PAINT

FRESH PAINT

New Poems by Eve Merriam

Woodcuts by David Frampton

Macmillan Publishing Company   New York

Macmillan Publishing Company
866 Third Avenue, New York, NY 10022
Collier Macmillan Canada, Inc.

Printed in the United States of America

10 9 8 7 6 5 4 3 2 1

The text of this book is set in 12 pt. Trump Medieval.
The illustrations are woodcuts.

Library of Congress Cataloging-in-Publication Data
Merriam, Eve, date.
Fresh paint.
Summary: Forty-five poems on subjects ranging from
the squat mushroom to the new moon.
1. Children's poetry, American. [1. American poetry]
I. Frampton, David, ill.   II. Title.
PS3525.E639F7   1986   811'.54   85-23742
ISBN 0-02-766860-6

To

the evergreen memory

of

Patricia Ayres

Fresh Paint

It glistens on this wall
that turns
whatever color I conjure
when I close my eyes:

green for the moss of
memories on a stone

blue for ice caves in August

scarlet for the banners of maple leaves
triumphant in the fall

yellow for the lights
of a homebound car in the fog

white for the drift of
cherry blossoms

orange for tiger flames
leaping in the bonfire

violet for daybreak
and violet for dusk

black for the warmth of darkness

and look
how the word *don't* is painted out
so the sign reads

    touch.

New Shoes

The first time in new shoes
my feet are encased
in wooden boats
so slippery
I can't even stay
afloat.

New Suit

A new suit is crackly
it smells like wrapping paper
and humiliates my old socks.

A New Pencil

The thing is,
you cannot write with it
until the point is sharpened
so turn it round and round

too few turnings
and the marks will be faint
too many
and the point will break

so turn and turn and
catch the wooden shavings
thin as soap slivers
my immigrant grandmother saved.

"You never know when bad times
are due to come round again;
besides, why waste anything?"
and so she saved and savored

the marrow in the meat bone at the bottom of the pot
the wilted tops of celery
chop them and start another simmering stew
that way the flame never has to go out

and in her sewing basket
ribbon from gift wrappings, bits of cloth,
lonely buttons, stray pieces of elastic;
what on earth for?

"You never know," she shrugs again,
"even with you and your friends growing up,
  the world's not perfect yet
  and if it needs stretching or holding together,

  well, here, here's a pencil,
  write something about it."

New Moon

Hold on to me.
We will slip carefully carefully
don't tip it over
into this canoe
pale as birch bark

and with the stars
over our shoulders
paddle
down the dark river
of the sky.

Do not delay.
By next week
the canoe will be bulging with cargo,
there will be no room
inside for us.

Tonight is the time.
Step carefully.
Hold on to me.

Flying for the First Time

Flying for the first time
the plane
is swimming in the sky

kicking up foamy clouds
riding the surf of clouds
cresting on waves of clouds.

Dive down
the foamy bubbles
break

the waves of the sky
recede
here is the tideline of

land.

On the First Snowfall

On the first snowfall
there is a pinhole
in the pillow of the sky

a feather
from a white dove
is falling from the sky

a petal
from a white rose
is falling from the sky

a tiny corner
of a page from a blank book
is falling from the sky

the petal
melts on my mouth
the feather
turns into a pen
and I write in the book
the silent word
      snow

I write it over and over
I write more words
secret words
scarlet words
greedy words
no one will know

the snow will cover my dreams.

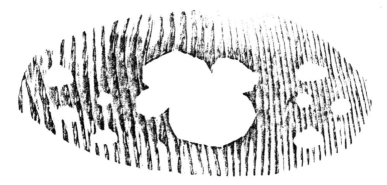

January Thaw

Puddles dry up,
kites fly up.

Gloves off,
mufflers doff.

Pedestrians out,
smiles sprout.

No need to wait
until July:

pass your plate now
for more sky pie.

The First Day of Spring

The first day of spring
itches
because
an emerald blade of grass
is
pushing out
of
my forehead

I've become
a unicorn.

Beyond Sci-Fi

Birds in the sea,
fish skyed above:
dream of the marvels
in worlds that may be.

Wake to the wonders
this world shows to me:
birds in the air,
fish in the sea.

Sunset

Yellow and pink as a peach
left to ripen on the tree

picked only at fullness
the circle of completion

and after it is consumed
we still savor the sweet perfume

and our fingers are stained
with golden and rose golden and rose

golden and rose
glowing into night.

Butterflies

Here, I've almost caught one!

Flitter flutter
Can't catch me, they tease. Can't catch me.

They play tag with us
leap into our hands
leak out like water

We lunge they laugh

They are fragments of gossip
on tiptoe we listen
What if? they flutter to each other. What if?

What if *what?*
but they're off in a dazzlement of air

Come back, we call out

Make a wish, they flicker like paper lanterns in the wind,
make a wish, and who knows
flitter flutter
their laughter floats up to the sky,
one day you may catch us after all
so try
      loop loft
             try
                loop loft again
                            try
                              try

try

Mushroom

Squat
it will never rule the world from on high

soft as eyelashes
soft
without even the memory of bones

its stem so gray it turns to silver

and smells more like the earth
than earth itself.

Quaking Aspen

The slightest breeze
orchestrates this tree
pianissimo
the leaves start up
their whispering music

the wind increases
emboldens
the leaves to timpani
agitato
agitato

the wind dies down
sotto voce the leaves
a silky violin
trembling for sorrow
trembling for joy.

Artichoke

Leaf
upon
layer
of
leaf
upon
layer
of
leaf
upon
layer
of
leaf
upon

The artichoke is the tortoise of vegetables.

From summer school it writes a letter home:

"Dear Parents,
        Yesterday we had a contest.
        Out of the whole class,
        I came in thirty-fourth.
        Hooray!"

Starfish

Its name linking
our farthest reaches
of sea
and sky

our age-old dream of attaining
highest
and
deepest

briny spiny asteroid
with four points for
the compass of our world
and the fifth

for galaxies
not yet
sailed
or flown to.

Giving Thanks Giving Thanks

Giving thanks giving thanks
for rain and rainbows
sun and sunsets
cats and catbirds
larks and larkspur

giving thanks giving thanks
for cows and cowslips
eggs and eggplants
stars and starlings
dogs and dogwood

giving thanks giving thanks
for watercress on river banks
for necks and elbows knees and shanks
for towers basins pools and tanks
for pumps and handles lifts and cranks

giving thanks giving thanks
for ropes and coils and braids and hanks
for jobs and jokes and plots and pranks
for whistles bells and plinks and clanks
giving giving giving *thanks*

Peeling an Orange

Tearing the skin carelessly
like yesterday's newspaper

or meticulously,
a carpenter restoring the spiral staircase in the castle

the juice
a rainspout gurgle

the smell
piercing the fog.

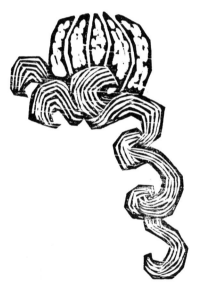

Fudging the Issue

A midge
nudged Madge
and left a smudge,
but Madge washed it off
and bears no grudge:
it could have been worse,
it could have been mucilage,
could have been sludge.

Strike Me Pink

Rose became madder,
she blushed,
flushed,
then "Grrr!" she said,
"I'm seeing red!"
Is it
cardinal,
tanager,
scarlet
or burgundy,
or is she that one in vermilion?

Excursion

A dancing bear at a summer fair
conversed with a jumping flea.

"It's hot and, ugh, the humidity,
my fur gets matted," complained the bear.

"I sorely agree, for I itch,"
said the flea.
"Shall we travel together
to cooler weather?
A breeze from the Arctic
might well be cathartic."

"Let's take it on the lam,"
declared the bear.
"Split, vamoose,
scat and skedaddle.
With no more ado,
let's be begone
to Seattle and Saskatchewan.
We could go as far north
as the Firth of Forth."

Said the flea with glee,
"We'll be refreshed and we can say
we wish each other an ice day."

Skip Rope Rhyme for Our Time

Junk mail, junk mail,
look look look:
bargain offer coupon,
catalogue book.

Junk mail, junk mail,
free free free:
trial sample,
guarantee.

Here's an offer
you can't let pass:
an artificial lawn
with real crab grass.

Twenty cents off,
just go to the store
and buy what you don't want,
then buy some more.

Junk mail, junk mail,
what's my name?
My name is Dear Occupant
and yours is the same.

Quest

When the landfills all are full,
and the oceans thick with slick,
where will we dump our waste:
will it have to be outer-spaced?

Will we put plastic bags on Jupiter?
Chemical tanks on the Milky Way?
Flammable trucks on Mars?
Dead batteries in the stars?

How to Solve a Problem

Crawl inside it
on your hands and knees

and give a good
substantial sneeze.

Notice to Myself

Don't procrastinate:
it's time to vacate
shilly-shallying
dilly-dallying
idling sidling
ambling rambling
piddling fiddling
twiddling diddling
doodling noodling
and get right down to
non-shirk
work.

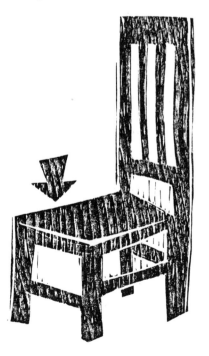

In the Park

Two old-timers
playing in the sun,
won't stop playing
till the chess game's won.

Two old-timers,
one moves a pawn;
the early morning warmth
is nearly gone.

Two old-timers
taking their time;
the bells of noon
begin to chime.

Two old-timers,
one moves a knight;
what has happened
to the afternoon light?

The swings and slides are empty,
the joggers jog on by,
the first star of evening
appears on high.

Checkmate, checkmate,
don't you dare,
two old-timers
still playing there.

Frame for a Picture

A haiku must contain
seventeen syllables exactly,
no more.

Idea:
to paint a picture with as few brush strokes
as possible.

Were I to try my hand,
I would use my haiku to say
I miss you.

Summer's End

In the still pond
the lily pads
rooted deep
as childhood memories.

Nothing moves.
Only a tiny ant
crawling across a rock.

Nowhere does the world
remain as it is.

New Love

I am telling my hands
not to blossom into roses

I am telling my feet
not to turn into birds
and fly over rooftops

and I am putting a hat on my head
so the flaming meteors
in my hair
will hardly show.

A Throw of Threes

Pillows

a cloud

a floor of ferns

a lap

Places to Hide a Secret Message

in a raindrop on a windowpane

in a moon shell

in a raisin in rice pudding

Apple Joys

twirling the star-shaped stem

biting into the ruddy globe

sliding out the satin seeds

Uses for Fog

to conquer skyscrapers

to make a magic cloak

to become thistledown

Anticipations

a crocus tip in the snow

the plume of a steam locomotive

an unopened letter

Lands Where No One Can Live

land without roots

land without the water of tears

land with no stones of loneliness

Cures for Melancholy

a barrel organ

a conversation with a mynah bird

a sprinkle of cinnamon inside your socks

Shimmerings

opalescent fins on a trout

the iridescent throat of a pigeon

a face glimpsed from a moving train

Places for an Extra Pocket

in a pelican's pouch

in a beard

in a fist

Curses to Fling at a Giant

May a gnat swallow you!

May a gnat swallow you and still be hungry!!

May a gnat step over you....

Silent Warnings

a moth at the screen door

a parachute

one glove

Disguises

an umbrella

a very polite yawn

a mirror

Questions for an Angel

Do you take it off when you go to sleep?

Do they fold back so you can put on a jacket?

Do you have memories?

Holidays

Somersault Eve

The Feast of Waterfall

Saint Chocolate's Day

Locked Doors

tomorrow
the heart of love
yourself

Open Doors

tomorrow
the heart of love
yourself